Zacchaeus

ILLUSTRATIONS BY CHANTAL MULLER VAN DEN BERGHE
TEXT BY BERNARD HUBLER

3

Distributed in the United Kingdom and Ireland by:
MATTHEW JAMES PUBLISHING Ltd
19 Wellington Close
Chelmsford, Essex CM1 2EE
Tel: 01245 347 710
Fax: 01245 347 713
ISBN 1-898366-24-1

Distributed in Canada by:
NOVALIS
49 Front St. E, 2nd Floor
Toronto, ON M5E 1B3
Tel: 1-800-387-7164
Fax (416 363-9409
ISBN 2-89088-937-8

Design: Jacques Rey

Gospel quotes are from Luke 19:1-10

*S*ometimes we can hardly remember what happened
    after we met someone for the first time.
But, at other times, the person we meet
    can make a very strong impression on us.
This is what happened to Zacchaeus when he met Jesus.
Jesus touched Zacchaeus' heart
    and his life changed for the better.
Wouldn't you want to have your life changed in this way?
Maybe you'll have an experience like this some day soon.
Meeting Jesus today is still possible.
Jesus still speaks to us as he did to Zacchaeus:

"Hurry down! I must stay at your house today!"

"Jesus entered Jericho and was passing through the city."

Jesus is on the street.
The street is full of life.
Jesus loves life.
He goes towards the crowd
and the crowd comes to meet him.

*To go towards others,
we must give of ourselves.*

"A man named Zacchaeus lived there."

Zacchaeus earned his living
as a tax collector.
He was very dishonest
and he tricked people
out of their money.
They disliked him
and called him a cheat.

*Some people try to cheat
rather than to play fairly.*

"He was trying to see Jesus, so he ran ahead of the crowd."

Zacchaeus was curious about Jesus
and wanted to see him,
but he was a little man
 and couldn't see because of the crowd.
  But Zacchaeus was crafty:
he always worked out
how to get what he wanted.

*There's always a way
to get around obstacles.*

"He climbed a sycamore tree."

Zacchaeus is comfortably perched in his tree.
He feels sheltered, hidden among the leaves.
Seeing things from above
he starts thinking about his life.

Taking time to think things over
can help us to see and to understand better.

"Jesus looked up and called out to him."

Jesus is at the foot of the tree
and Zacchaeus is up in the branches.
This is a special moment for Zacchaeus.
Deep down, more than anything else, he wants to meet Jesus.
Jesus knows this and looks up at Zacchaeus.

If you really want to meet someone,
you mustn't go rushing around.

"Hurry down!
I must stay at your house today."

To welcome Jesus to his house,
Zacchaeus must climb down from the tree.
However, he must also come down
from the tree inside himself:
the tree of his pride and of his lack of concern for others.

*If you think you are better
than other people,
or if you don't care about them,
they'll never want to be with you.*

"He welcomed Jesus with great joy."

Zacchaeus gets his house ready.
He is very honoured
to receive Jesus into his home.
He invites Jesus for supper.
Zacchaeus is very happy.

We don't invite just anybody to our home.
Friendship can develop by sharing a meal.

"The people who saw it began to grumble and said:

'He has gone as a guest to the home of a sinner.'"

Jesus went to eat with someone whom everyone else thought was a sinner. People were shocked and they criticized Jesus severely.

Only people who do nothing are never criticized.

"I will give half of my belongings to the poor."

Because Jesus spent time with him,
Zacchaeus is no longer the same.
He decides to make up for the things he has done.
He has discovered something
that money can't buy:
the happiness of being loved.
From now on he will try to do good.

Happy are they who know they are loved:
their life will be changed.

"Today salvation has come to this house."

Jesus didn't arrive yesterday
and no one has to wait until tomorrow.
He's here today in Zacchaeus' house.
Today happiness has arrived through Jesus.
Today everything has changed.

Love can't wait for tomorrow.
We must show our love to others
today.

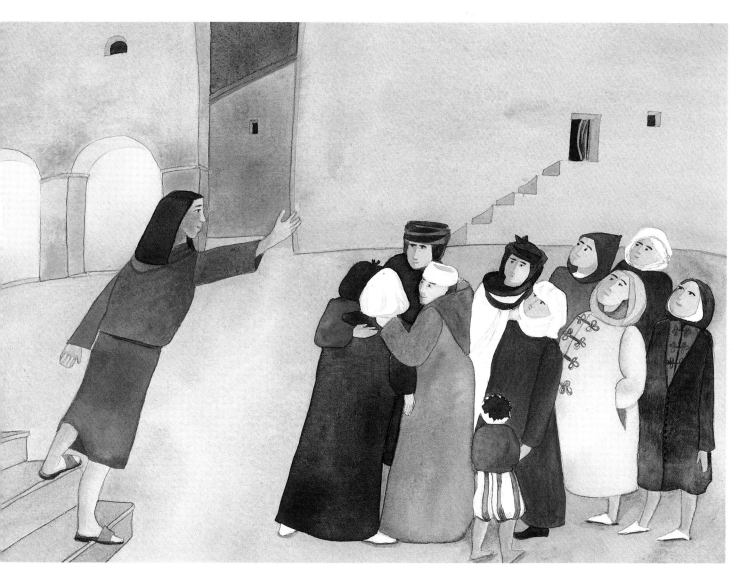

As you were reading this book,
did it help you to see
that the things Jesus did
and the words he said
are addressed to you today?
When someone is with you in a special way
you'll never be exactly the same again.
Being together in this way changes something in our life.
Sometimes our whole life is completely changed.
But this won't happen if you behave like a turtle
which keeps hiding in its shell.
You have to open your heart today to welcome
the One who invites himself into your home.

"Jesus entered Jericho and was passing through the city."

"A man named Zac-chaeus lived there."

6

8

"He was trying to see Jesus, so he ran ahead of the crowd."

"He climbed a sycamore tree."

10

12

"Jesus looked up and called out to him."

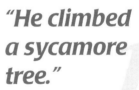

16

14

"Hurry down! I must stay at your house today."

"The people who saw it began to grumble and said: 'He has gone as a guest to the home of a sinner.'"

"Today salvation has come to this house."

"He welcomed Jesus with great joy."

"I will give half of my belongings to the poor."

In the same
collection:

Bartimaeus
The Good Samaritan
The Paralysed Man
The Calming of the Storm
The Prodigal Son
The Call of the Disciples
Shared Bread
The Amazing Catch
The Forgiven Sinner
The Sower
The Disciples from Emmaus